Table for One

and Other Poems

by Jenni Finlay

Illustrations and Cover Design
by Marc Harkness

First Edition, 2015
Copyright © 2015 by Jenni Finlay
All Rights Reserved.

ISBN-13: 978-0-9837383-3-6
Library of Congress Control Number:
2015930591

No part of this book may be performed, recorded, or otherwise transmitted without the written consent of the author and the permission of the publisher. However, portions of poems may be cited for book reviews—favorable or otherwise—without obtaining consent.

Cover Design: Marc Harkness
Illustrations: Marc Harkness
Back Cover Photo: Brian T. Atkinson

Mezcalita Press, LLC
Norman, Oklahoma

Table for One

and Other Poems

by Jenni Finlay

... For Brian ...

who encouraged me to "fucking write"
and kept me mostly sane.

Table of Contents

Acknowledgements viii
Foreword ix

Preface 2
Almost 4
Boob Tube 6
Floors 7
Pigeon Holes 8
Uncle Tommy 10
The Smell of Success 11
Rebecca 12
Poem from Denver 14
The Picnic Tablers 16
Transplant 18
Caffeine 20
Caregiver. Caretaker 21
Chapel 23
Early Bird Special 25
Turn Turn Turn 27
Lucky Charms 29
Doctor Marx 31
One Week Down, Two to Go 32
The Black-Eyed Pea 33
The Wailing Woman of 303 34
Onward through the Fog 36
Calm.Down. 38

Table for One 40
Lunch Break 42
Burn Whatever's Left 44
Last Night 47
Checking Out 50

Author Bio 53
Illustrator Bio 54

Acknowledgements

Special thanks to Dad for the incredible journey, Clay for his strong and loving shoulder, Mom for her perspective and amazing support, Nathan and Ashley for their inspiration and encouragement.

Big thanks to my family for my strength, and my friends for theirs.

Thanks to all who came down to fill my table and my heart: Clay McNeill, Diana Hendricks, Sage and Briannon Allen, Brian T. and Suzie Atkinson, Jan Clark, Curtis McMurtry, Nathan and Ashley Brown, Kellie Salome, and James McMurtry.

FOREWORD

Jenni Finlay writes earthy poetry straight from the heart. She pulls no punches. Adds no frills. Jenni's poems are raw and real and completely unspoiled by the bad deal life doubled down on her father and family. Her words move in every sense. They roll like thunderclouds and rain and every nuance behind healing and pain. Turn the page. You'll learn life lessons in care and compassion and calling your own heart into action.

Jenni allowed a most uncommon pleasure during this impossible journey: She sent me these words in real time as she wrote them. Every night she sliced her day with clear eyes. Every night another poem would come through. Her snapshots were devastating and disarming. Upending and uplifting. Occasionally uproarious. These pages are filled with vibrant internal monologues equally heartbreaking and heartening. Jenni simply wrote what she witnessed and her poems frame a time and place with unflinching honesty. They're objective and ominous and omnipresent.

I visited Jenni one afternoon during this time and I can tell you with no doubt: Her words are true life in motion. They effortlessly capture the tenderness and terror hanging in the air around that hospital and hotel. We all like to think we could accept the same challenge she did. Honestly, I'm not sure I could have handled the daily battering. Jenni's tears every night when we spoke on the phone made immediate sense as I pulled up to her room. The first thing I saw was a door wide open four rooms down. A woman lay sprawled lifelessly across her bed openly weeping. Screaming. Shouting. Swearing at the gods and anyone passing by. Her heartbreak owned absolutely no shelter. Meanwhile, everyone else was drinking liquor by the common area barbecue grill. I looked at my watch: Four minutes until noon. Jesus Christ.

Thank you, Jenni, for sharing these stories. They're captivating and courageous and count every blessing unearthed in moments when all the cards were down. As our pal wrote, you have the guts and gasoline. Keep writing. You're onto something here.

– Brian T. Atkinson, author of *I'll Be Here in the Morning: The Songwriting Legacy of Townes Van Zandt*.

TABLE FOR ONE

Preface

Outback Steakhouse…
Nothing is open on Sunday evenings
except chain joints and Chinese buffets.
I pull in and ask for a table for one.
I sit cross-legged with my leather journal
in front of me and study the menu.
The bread hasn't changed in sixteen years.
In my head, I'm suddenly in mid-
conversation with a long-lost friend.
We'd make plans to change the world
at restaurants with good bread.
Good bread was a must.
This was our favorite.
French onion soup seems appropriate.
It was the only thing I could eat last time
Dad was going through all this.

I would make my own.

(Worchestershire is the secret.)

I haven't eaten it in almost eleven years.

As the first bite slightly burns my tongue,

I feel the whoosh of flashback—instant

sensory recollection. Except not really.

I'm here. The soup is real. Dad has cancer.

This is more than a memory.

Almost

My motel room's very pleasant.
I replaced the bedspread
with my old, tattered
high school quilt.

No bad art on the wall.
My kitchenette has a full-sized fridge
and there's a door mat
and a picnic area across the way.

You could almost call it charming.

Boob Tube

Available TV Channels:

HBO

HBO 2

HBO Spec

CNN

TNT

ESPN 2

PORN

PORN

PORN

FLOORS

The hospital floors
are made out of shiny
fake wood-grain laminate.

For wheelchairs, I suppose.
Makes me wish I had roller skates.

Pigeon Holes

We watch pigeons find their homes
in the funky cinderblock grid
covering the hospital's side walls.

They constantly fly in and out,
off to work and home again
from their busy pigeon lives.

Oblivious to what's going on here.
There are times I envy them.

Uncle Tommy

Tommy spoke up today
after spending hours
staring at the IV machine
rhythmically pumping poison
into Dad's veins.

"Isn't it amazing the stuff
we've found to treat all this?
We should really thank
those white rats."

THE SMELL OF SUCCESS

Dad reeks of garlic-flavored chemicals
from breathing out the preservatives
that have been keeping his harvested
stem cells fresh for the transplant.

You can smell him down the hall—
"the smell of success"
the nurses call it.

He doesn't even notice.
Kinda like the people
who live in Luling.

Rebecca

Lorenzo's is a tiny Italian joint
in a strip center catty-cornered
to my motel with a laundromat,
hair design studio, and the Pressure
Cooker Cocktail Bar.
Hardly anyone else ever eats here.
The boss yelled at the brand-new waitress
the first day I came here,
and she was almost fired.
I tipped ten bucks on a twenty-dollar tab.
Now I sit in her section every night.
Her name's Rebecca, but she looks
like my friend Lori, who is also a waitress.
Rebecca, my only friend in town,
pours the wine I like before I ask.
She always asks about Dad.

Poem From Denver

Stuffed in between the pages
of *Writing Down The Bones*
is a poem Brian wrote for me
on five napkins at the Satire Lounge
in Denver at noon last Tuesday.

That day seems like a world
away and forever ago.
I should have left the poem at home,
had it framed and hung it in my office,
but it snuck itself here like a stowaway.

I'm glad I have it.
It's about being different now
in a world that's stayed the same.

He's currently answering my emails,
doing my radio charts and dealing
with the people I really don't
want to deal with.
Things I will never
be able to repay.

There are people in this world
who will take the heart out of you.
And there are those who put it back.

The Picnic Tablers

They sit there all afternoon
and well into the night.
Even though she's probably a local,
I call the small firecracker Jersey Girl.
She looks like Marisa Tomei.
She sits with her hulky boyfriend,
grandma, and skater-boy nephew.
They have a four-year-old
terrier named Stella.
They're loud and rowdy,
inviting and friendly
and shout "hellooo!"
across the parking lot whenever
I set up my red plastic lawn chair
outside my door. You'd think
they were on vacation.

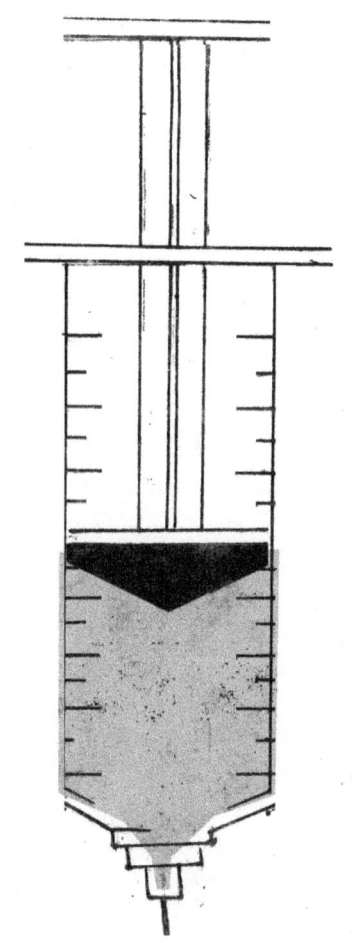

Transplant

Here we go:
The fat syringe slowly plunging.
Thick deep-red stem cells
surge through his veins.

O-negative. 2-9-38.
They've gone over his information
aloud twice. *Kent Finlay... errr...*
I mean James Kent Finlay.
We're nervous.
Seems like a test.

He winces and Nurse Angela stops.
"We can take a break. Are you okay?"
He squeezes his eyes shut,

tears spilling out. "Yes…"
he whispers, unconvincingly,
his face and neck flushed red.

"Do you have an ice-cream headache?"
I ask, not knowing how else to describe it.
Even though I'm trying to be helpful,
I feel like I'm in the way.
"It's okay. Keep going.
Get it over with."

Caffeine

I'm back on caffeine.
Went off after panic attacks
a few months ago.

I cracked my first Diet Coke
in two months, the day
we started the transplant.

The bottle instructed me
to share it with my buddy Rob.
I thought that was kinda pushy,

but I went ahead and drank half,
then texted a picture to him.

CAREGIVER. CARETAKER

Huh.

I'm not sure which either.

Chapel

I look for the fancy cappuccino machine
but find the hospital's chapel instead.
I walk in, intrigued.

The heavy doors aren't inviting;
they slam if you're not careful
(this is not a chapel you can
slip into mid-service).

It's empty when I wander in,
extremely quiet and reminiscent
of a fancy hotel lobby with big
plush chairs instead of pews.

A cradle-Episcopalian,
I pull out a kneeler

from under the altar
and set it in the second row
(left-side, naturally).

I sit for a while.
I pray for a while,
my father's Agnosticism
my main concern.

Before I leave,
I even fill out a prayer card,
for professional Methodists
to work on later.

Early Bird Special

I get to the Chinese Buffet a little before five.
Just in time for the Early Bird Special.
Beef with Garlic Sauce. I look around
as I pour the hot oil. We're all
in the same (sushi) boat.

The waitress comes by
and refills my tea
and offers me
the medical discount.

I don't have to ask.

Turn Turn Turn

He mans the motel grill,
slowly turning the hot dogs
and sausages he's constantly cooking.

He's said his goodbyes. He's resigned,
said all there is to say. No regrets.
Just waiting for the call now.

He waves us over, offering his delicious
franks to anyone who wanders by.
"There's plenty to go around,"
he says, smiling.

Lucky Charms

Turquoise suede bookmark

with a peacock feather.

Hopalong Cassidy toy gun

Case pocketknife

Lion paw lapel pin

Large black snail shell

Townes Van Zandt guitar pick

Peso

Coupon from the '88 State Fair of Texas

Piece of Red Rocks

Doctor Marx

Our daily doctor looks
and sounds like Groucho Marx.
He talks fast and has the moustache
and the hair. "You have a fever?
That's perfectly normal. Pain?
Absolutely normal. Swelling? No?
Huh. You should be swelling more."
He'd be funnier with the cigar.

One Week Down, Two to Go

One foot in front of the other
One foot in front of the other
One foot in front of the other

The Black-Eyed Pea

They serve cheap wine in heavy pours
at noon on Thursday.
Everything overcooked, over-
salted, over-the-edges of the plate.
He looks around oblivious and says,
"This was Mom's favorite restaurant
before she died."
I nod slowly in sad agreement.

The Wailing Woman of 303

She rooms at the end of the building.
She props her door open
with the big ugly motel club chair.
She lays across her bed,
her freckled legs paled
by the stream of sunlight.
Day in. Day out.
Sobbing uncontrollably.

Onward Through The Fog

"The doctors say I'm not going to start
feeling bad until tomorrow," Dad says.
We're sitting almost knee to knee
in straight-backed chairs.
"See?" I say, triumphantly,
"They first thought it would be yesterday!
You're an overachiever."
He stares at me. Blinks.
Stares hard and blinks again.
I think he's mad, but I concentrate
on his face and wait. His face
loses all color. "All I see is a white fog
in front of where you should be,"
he whispers, and rubs his eyes
behind his glasses.
I press the button, step out

and grab Nurse Jackie.
60/40 blood pressure.
Incredible excitement.
Everyone comes in to look.
They carry him to the bed
and hook him to many machines.
"I guess I'm an overachiever,"
he jokes, half-heartedly.

CALM.DOWN.

Last night I lost my fucking mind.
In one fell swoop, I attempted
to drive away my closest friend—
the one man who has done the most
to help me through it all.
I was angry, lonely, scared, cruel.
I was not myself and the most
myself I've ever been.
I awoke with tears in my eyes,
awfully certain I had surrendered
our friendship like his treasured
pocketknife at airport security.
But the familiar early morning text
came through without hesitation.
Like always: AM. What's the plan?
Turns out his friendship endures.

It's mightier than me at my worst,
tougher than my anger,
bigger than my loneliness,
stronger than my fears.
I don't understand friends.

Table for One

I'm underdressed,
maybe overwhelmed.
Either way,
no one says anything.
But I don't quite fit.
This place is for celebrations,
Birthdays and bar mitzvahs,
families and friends. They
rehearse First Communion rites,
discuss bridesmaid choices.
Grandpa slips the children
their first nip of wine and laughs.
A new mother rushes out,
muting her wailing infant
in the crook of her arm.
They fight over who gets

to tell a favorite story.
They fight over where they
should take their next vacation.
They fight over who
gets to pay the ticket.
The piano player plays
"White Christmas,"
even though it's July.
I do not belong here right now.

Lunch Break

We need to find someone to sub
this month for the regular Tuesday gig.
That sponsor money needs to clear
the bank before the hotel bill breaks it.
The band leaves for Canada Wednesday
and the bass player's passport is expired.
(When it rains, it pours!) Working fast,
I crank out the emails, get on the phone,
put out the fires. Damn it's good to be back,
I think, finally feeling like myself again,
back in the swing of things.
My phone buzzes.
I grab it and gulp down the Diet Coke,
enjoying its slow burn down my throat.
"You really have to talk to the nurses.
They brought the wrong pudding again.

And I must have my other pants
as soon as possible."
I feel my shoulders slump
as I slowly shut the lid to my laptop,
click off the light
and rush out the door.

Burn Whatever's Left

He shouldn't have answered the phone.
She told him it was because
she wanted him to know.
He NEEDED to know.
Everyone else would deny it
if he asked because he's so
sensitive and everyone
protects him from bad news.
"Don't tell anyone I told you…"
she said, secretively…
Before she moved away,
she felt it was her responsibility
to tell him that his father
had only two weeks to live.
It was cruel and hurtful,
untruthful, and very much

like something she would do.
It's not enough to burn bridges.
She wants the whole village
ablaze as she's leaving town.
This is her legacy.

Last Night

The ruckus pulls us away
from the glowing laptops,
the boob tubes, the grill
and picnic tables.
We rush outside.
The Wailing Woman of 303
tears through the night, banging
her fists across all our car hoods
like an AK-47, her sobs
bellowing into the charcoal sky.
We stand paralyzed, helplessly watching.
Jersey Girl's boyfriend screams forward
and wraps her up in his massive arms.
"It's okay, Mama. It's okay."
He holds her tight.
She crumbles,

broken to the bone,

heart emptied dry.

"My daughter's DEAD,"

she chokes out.

We carry her to the picnic table

then immediately rush

booze in from every room:

Whiskey. Vodka. Beer. Wine.

She pours a vodka.

Says her daughter was

twenty-two, smart and funny.

She slams the drink. Whiskey.

Now she's dead. Vodka. Heart disease.

Rum. Beer chaser. She looks to the sky.

Points toward her glass.

We keep pouring her another

and another and another, the bottles

hardly touching the table until

we've numbed her to sleep.

We put her back in bed

and drag ourselves back

to our own rooms.

Wounded. Guilty. Thankful.

Thank the lord –

Thank you, Jesus! –

we're not her.

Thank you.

We're. Not. Her.

We pour our next rounds alone.

Checking Out

I fold up my quilt.
Carefully pack up my lucky charms.
Throw out the antibacterial gel.
I walk down to the front office
for the last time.
The woman behind me in line
is on the phone.
"I just got here," she says.
"We haven't gotten the official diagnosis,
but they think it's childhood leukemia."
I quietly lay my plastic keycard on the desk,
turn and walk out the door,
leaving this place behind.
(I hope.)

Author

Jenni Finlay co-authored the forthcoming *Kent Finlay, Dreamer* (Texas A&M University Press, 2016) and served as contributing writer for *Pickers and Poets: The Ruthlessly Poetic Singer-Songwriters of Texas* (Texas A&M University Press, 2016). She co-owns Eight 30 Records and co-produced the forthcoming tribute album *Cold and Bitter Tears: The Songs of Ted Hawkins* (2015). Her Jenni Finlay Promotions business has shaped careers for several dozen iconic Americana music singer-songwriters for the past decade. Finlay presents the monthly series Catfish Concerts, which will release *Catfish Concerts Cookbook: Celebrating Americana's Finest Recipes* (Mezcalita Press, LLC, 2016).

ILLUSTRATOR

Marc Harkness is a designer, illustrator, and musician currently residing in Asheville, North Carolina. Born and raised in the Republic of Panama, Marc has designed packaging and posters for Billy Joe Shaver, James McMurtry, the Steep Canyon Rangers, Sarah Lee Guthrie and Johnny Irion, among others. When not at work, he is at play, running and kayaking in the Blue Ridge Mountains.

www.ingramcontent.com/pod-product-compliance
Lightning Source LLC
Chambersburg PA
CBHW051715040426
42446CB00008B/902